Wǒ Shì Dào

I AM the Way

Because the path of liberation has and always will be inward

我
是
道

Li Vej

"The Farmer and the Horse"
(Good isn't always good and bad isn't always bad)

They came to him shouting,
"Your horse is gone! Misfortune!"

But the old man only stirred the dust with his toe,

And said, "How do you know it is misfortune?"

Days passed. The horse returned
Not alone but with wild companions.

Now they praised him, "Fortune smiles on you, old one!"

But he sipped his tea and said, "How do you know it is fortune?"

The next day
one of the wild horses threw his son
The boy's leg bent where no leg should. The neighbors wailed
again,

But the old man only knelt in prayer.

"The truth is not finished yet," he said. "It only speaks in whole
circles."

Then came the war. And all the young were taken
Except the limping boy, who could not march.

And the villagers whispered: "Perhaps he sees what we do not."

But the old man never smiled.
He only watched the wind and answered nothing. Because he knew
What breaks you may bless you. What blesses you may chain you.
And naming something too soon is how suffering begins.

Author: Same for those who love too far before it's becoming

Reflection / Notes

Reflection / Notes

Author
Li Vej,

BEFORE WE BEGIN

This is not a book about finding answers. It is a book about discovering the questions you've always carried. The ones that ache in your bones and whisper in the quiet between heartbeats. For years, I searched for peace in philosophies, in religions, in the silent corners of libraries and the loud corners of the world. I found wisdom everywhere but stillness nowhere. Until I realized I was looking in the wrong place. I was looking out when I was always in.

This book is a map of that inward journey but it is not a map made of lines and destinations. It is made of breath, parable and poetry. It is built on a single, practical truth: Between what you feel and what you do, there is a space. In that space, you are free.

The exercises you'll find here are not about emptying your mind or rising above your emotions. They are about becoming fluent in the language of your own body; about using your breath to build a sanctuary within, so you can feel everything without being swept away. This is the practice of emotional sovereignty. It is the art of standing in the storm without becoming the storm.

Here, you will not be told to "let go" of your pain. You will be shown how to hold it, how to listen to it and how to let it transform you; without letting it define you. We will walk through parables old and new, through verses that feel like remembered prayers and through breaths that steady the soul. This is not a path of more knowledge but of deeper remembrance. You already know the way. You have just forgotten how to listen. So, let us begin where all real journeys start: With a single, conscious breath.

THE FIRST BREATH: Why Everything Begins Here!

Close your eyes for a moment. Feel the air entering your body. Notice the pause before it leaves. That pause is where your life happens. Most of us breathe without thinking. We pant when we're scared, we hold our breath when we're hurt, we sigh when we're weary. Our breath becomes a reaction, a shadow of our emotions; following fear, anger, or grief like a servant but what if you could reverse that? What if your breath could become the guide? Think of the last time you were truly upset. Your breath was likely short, shallow and tight. That kind of breathing doesn't calm the storm, it feeds it. It tells your brain you are in danger, even when you are safe. It clouds your thoughts, tightens your body and leaves you feeling trapped inside your own reaction. That is reactive breath. It is what happens when emotion is in charge.

The breathwork in this book is different. It is a conscious breath.
It is how you take back the reins. The Science of the Pause

When you are overwhelmed, you may feel like you are gasping for air but that kind of rapid, panicked breathing is surprisingly inefficient. It upsets the delicate balance of oxygen and carbon dioxide in your blood. Which can actually reduce oxygen flow to your brain. This is why we feel dizzy, scattered and disconnected when we are highly emotional.

Conscious, rhythmic breathing restores that balance. It signals directly to your nervous system: You are safe, You can handle this, It gives your brain the clarity it needs to feel without flooding.

This is not avoiding emotion. This is honoring it with the space it deserves. The Bridge Between Feeling and Freedom! Every emotion is a kind of energy. Anger is heat. Grief is weight. Joy is light. Fear is tension.

When that energy arises, you have a choice: You can let it move through you, or you can let it move you. Without the anchor of the breath, emotion moves you, it becomes the sharp word you regret. The withdrawal you didn't mean, the decision made in panic.

With the breath as your anchor, you let emotion move through you. You feel the heat of anger without letting it become a wildfire. You feel the weight of grief without letting it pull you under. In that space, the space between feeling and acting. Your freedom lives and your breath is the key to that space.

What This Means for Your Life

When you learn to breathe with intention, you change more than your inner world. You change how you meet the outer one; You stop wearing masks for others; You stop bending your truth to fit someone else's expectations; You stop handing your peace over to every passing opinion or criticism; You become grounded. Present. Accountable. You become someone who can listen deeply, love openly and stand firmly. Not because you are perfect but because you are rooted in your own being. And in that rootedness, you become someone others can truly rely on because you are no longer asking them to steady you. You are offering them a steady hand instead.

This is the foundation of real love. Not the love that demands
but the love that offers. Not the love that clings but the love that stands firm. It all begins with a breath. One conscious, chosen breath.

HOW TO USE THIS BOOK

This book is built in three repeating layers:
1. A Parable – A short story to illuminate a truth.
Read it like a mirror. See what reflects back.
2. A Verse – A poetic meditation to carry the truth
from your head to your heart. Let it settle in your bones.
3. A Breath – A simple exercise to embody the truth in your body.

This is where knowing becomes being.

You do not need to read this book in order. You do not need to finish it quickly. When a parable speaks to you, stay there. When a breath comforts you, return to it. Let the book be a companion, not a task.

This is not about information. It is about transformation. And transformation moves at the speed of breath.

A FINAL WORD: My hope is that these pages offer you what I most needed when I began: not another theory but a practice. Not another voice telling you who to be but a way to remember who you are.

In bringing together wisdom from many traditions:

Daoist, Zen, Stoic, Christian, Indigenous and more.
I have sought only what is universal: the human longing for peace,
the courage to feel deeply and the breath that carries us home.
Walk gently. Breathe deeply. Remember.You are already the Way.
Ready to begin?

Turn the page and take your first conscious breath.

Table of Contents
Wǒ Shì Dào 我是道 I Am the Way

Part VI: The Final Note\Breath Work: Lion's Breath
Part VII: The Last Gift\Breath Work: The Emotional Anchor

Part 0   Wise Uncertainty
Breathe work: Letting Go Breath

Breathe the Grain Away
"The Breath of Perspective"

How to Practice:
Inhale slowly through the nose, gathering what you carry.
Hold gently
Acknowledge the weight.
Exhale with a whispered "haaaah" through the mouth.

Repeat:
Inhale (4) → Hold (2) → Exhale (6)
Do this for 5 minutes or until your spirit softens.
Prompt: One breath is enough.
One grain of truth is enough.
You were never too small   just too heavy.

Breath Pattern:
Inhale (4) → Hold (2) → Exhale (6)
Repeat for 5 minutes

This breath is for letting go what doesn't belong to you.
Practice it in silence.
Let each exhale be a goodbye to control. You don't need to grasp the whole. One
grain of truth is enough.

What to Let Go: The illusion of "too small to matter."
The need to grasp the whole.
The fear that silence means nothingness.

What to Hold On To:
One breath. One truth.
One grain of the infinite.
Reflection: This is perspective. Not giving up   letting be.

000 The Sand Grain Truth (Parable)

A Bedouin wanderer once crossed a vast desert with nothing but a pouch of dates and
a flask of water. As he walked, the wind picked up and stung his face with sand. He
bent down, scooped a single grain from the dune and held it to the sun.

"This," he said,
"is truth small, sharp, mine to keep."

He tucked it in his pouch as if it were treasure.
But as the days went on, his pouch grew heavy.
He filled it with handfuls of sand,
each grain another "truth" he believed he must carry.
By the third day, the pouch ripped,
spilling everything back to the desert floor.
Exhausted, the wanderer fell to his knees.
That night, in a dream, he saw the desert itself speak:
"Foolish one. Truth cannot be carried in a pouch. It cannot be weighed, divided, or
kept for yourself. A grain may remind you but it is not the whole. The whole is the
dune, the dunes are the desert and the desert is without end."
The wanderer woke with empty hands. For the first time, he felt no need to collect.
He stood and looked out across the endless sands,
and in the vastness he no longer feared being lost. He walked on
not with truth in his pouch but truth in his sight.
And from then on, whenever the wind carried sand against his face,
he did not curse it. He let the grains sting his skin,
for they reminded him: to try and possess truth is to be buried by it,
but to walk within it is to be free.

So he walked on,
light as the wind, no longer a man who gathered truths,
but one who was gathered by the desert itself.

Verse 0
The Sand Grain Truth

For me truth
was a grain of sand
a fact, a piece I could pocket,
carry like a credential granted by God

But what is truth or reality if it's only mine
just a sliver, a shimmer, a fraction
mistaking itself for the full light.

Truth is more than sand in a sandbox or the beach, the dunes, the desert
it cannot be divided and still be called whole or true.

What we call truth
is just a piece we've broken off and worshipped as the whole.
What we call reality is the shadow of a mountain seen from inside a cave.
What we call meaning is the thread we spin to keep pain from unraveling.

Emotions may show us truth but emotions are not reality.
It's merely a sensor or the lenses in which we see ourselves in
an illusion among illusions.

But of all the emotional lies we build, love is the one we win on.
It binds the grains together.
It gives the shifting dunes a shape worth walking.

If I must lie to myself, let it be in love.
If I must wander this mirage, let me
carry what is noble and more lasting than the body I've been given

Let the grain fall. Let it scatter.

But I will walk
not to find the truth,
but to carry the lie that can make the
meaningless
meaningful

Reflection / Notes

Part I Empty Hands
Breathe work: The Soft Releasing Breath

Let the Grain Fall
"The Breath that Holds and Releases"

How to Practice:
Breathe out through your mouth softly for 4 counts.
Hold for 4 counts again.
Let your jaw relax. Let your breath be quiet. Tongue should rest gently behind your
top teeth.
Prompt: With each breath, picture a single grain of sand falling from your hand.
You are not losing truth   you are becoming light enough to walk in it.
Let the pause between breaths be your teacher. In the stillness, you remember.

Breath Pattern:
Inhale (4) → Hold (4) → Exhale (4) → Hold (4)
Repeat for 3 5 rounds, or until you feel release.
This breath is about surrender, ease and emotional unburdening.
Inhale slowly through the nose for a count of four, feeling the ribs expand.
Hold gently don't clench, just hover.
Then exhale audibly through the mouth with a sigh for a count of six.
Repeat for several minutes. Visualize a leaf falling gently from a tree.
Every breath out is a layer of expectation, tension, or identity dropping away. This can
be practiced seated or lying down. Let your belly be soft, your jaw relaxed. Allow
yourself to feel silly if needed softness is a form of courage. Practice this breath when
you're stuck in the "shoulds" or holding back tears. It's a quiet release. This isn't
about power it's about peace. Give yourself permission to loosen your grip.

What to Let Go:
The pressure to arrive or prove.
All the fake strength that came from pretending.
The identity you wore to survive but no longer need.

What to Hold On To:
Your innocence. The breath that empties without fear.
The space in your palm where something real might land.
Reflection: This is surrender. Not weakness   readiness.
Empty hands aren't empty… they're finally open.

001   The Illusion of Freedom (Parable)

In the crowded marketplace of Rome,
a philosopher named Epictetus once lived as a slave.
The people who passed him in chains pitied him, yet he pitied them more.
For though they walked freely through the streets,
he saw their minds bound tighter than any shackle.

One day, a master, testing him, twisted his leg.
Epictetus did not cry out, only said calmly:
"If you continue, you will break it." The master pressed harder and the bone snapped.
Epictetus looked up and said: "And now, it is broken."

The master laughed, thinking him conquered.
Yet in that silence, Epictetus had already walked beyond his chains.
His freedom was not of the body but of the mind, not of permission but of perception.

Later, his students asked, "How can a man in chains speak of freedom?" And he told
them a parable:
"A bird in a cage may be envied by another who flies above but if the bird sings, if it
turns its gaze toward heaven, then it belongs to no master. The body is a cage, yes but
freedom is the song. Do not confuse movement with liberty, or ownership with
belonging. The one who rules his own mind cannot be enslaved."

And so his chains became his teacher, his broken leg his scripture. He learned that
most men are imprisoned not by iron but by desire:
desire for wealth, desire for approval, desire for power. What master is harsher than
the hunger that is never filled?

The students looked around at the bustling streets, the senators, the generals, the
merchants, each chained to gold, to fear, to pride.
And they understood. The slave was freer than the empire that claimed to own him.

For freedom is not given, nor stolen, nor decreed.
Freedom is the recognition that nothing external can command your soul.

Verse 1
The Illusion of Freedom

They spoke of freedom
as if it were a treasure to be won
a pearl at the bottom of the sea,
a prize for those who dive deepest.

But I was born already clothed
not in silk but in
stories, names, flags, fears
woven into my flesh
before I had words to protest.

Did I choose this name? This sorrow? This soil?

Or was I planted like a seed
by hands I do not remember
told to bloom in a garden I never chose?

Still…
I stretch toward the light.
Not because I am free,
but because the seed knows no other way.

Freedom is not escape
it is presence.

Not in the fleeing but in the being.
The master walks not without chains,
but with grace in their weight.

He bows
to the illusion and still walks on

002   And The Names we Shed(Parable)

There was once a man named
Saul who walked with thunder in his chest.

Every step he took cracked the earth, for he believed he alone carried truth.
He was fire without water, sword without sheath.
His eyes cut men down before his hands ever touched them.

But on the road to Damascus, the heavens struck him blind.
No lightning touched him, yet all the world grew dark. He fell to his knees,
not because he wished to,
but because pride cannot stand when the universe closes its eyes.

In the silence of blindness, Saul heard not accusation but a question:
"Why do you strike at Me, when I have never struck at you?"

The voice was not thunder, nor whisper but both.
It carried the weight of stars collapsing and the gentleness of a mother's breath.
Saul wept, for the first time seeing what eyes could not.
And when he rose, he was no longer Saul the Destroyer,
but Paul the Broken, Paul the Reborn.

The world did not change
he did.
And because he did, the world could. For every soul must die before it lives:
the wolf must be slain, the seed must be buried, the fire must burn itself into ash
so that the green shoot may push through, so that new light may dawn.
Thus Saul's blindness was his birth and his name was his grave.

The man who thought he carried truth was carried instead by it.
And the thunder in his chest became rain,
soft enough to heal the scorched earth he once burned.

Verse 2
And The Names We Shed

To name a thing
is to place it in a box
to dress the infinite in robes
too tight for truth.

They called me many things:
son, student, sinner, saint.

Each name a mirror
but none showed my face.

I wore them like borrowed cloaks,
trying to feel warmth in someone else's fabric.
But the more I tried to belong,
the more I vanished.

The Self is not a statue
to be worshipped
it is a river
and the river laughs at the idea of being held.

So I let the names fall,
like leaves in autumn.

I let go of who I was told to be,
to become
what I had always been.

Not a title. Not a mask. But a breath,
a presence.

a question that doesn't need
answering.

003 The Illusion of Ownership (Parable)

An elder once gathered the children of the village beneath the great cedar.
He set down a bundle of soil, black and fragrant, tied up in a piece of cloth.
"Tell me," he said,
"whose earth is this?" The children laughed. "It is yours, Elder!" "No it is ours!"
One boy, bold and eager, stood tall.
"If I build a fence around it, then it will belong to me."
The elder nodded. "Take it then."
The boy untied the cloth, scooped the soil into his hands and clutched it to his chest.
At first he grinned, proud of his possession.
But the earth slipped through his fingers, crumbling, scattering.
He pressed harder but the tighter he held, the less remained.
Soon only dust streaked his skin.
The elder spread his palms toward the cedar.
"Did the boy own the soil? Or did the soil own him?"
The children were silent.
He went on:
"The river feeds the fish, the fish feed the bear, the bear feeds the earth again.
Who owns whom? The cedar grows not because one claims it,
but because the sun gives without asking. To say mine is to forget you are only
borrowing."
One girl raised her hand. "Then nothing belongs to us?"
The elder smiled.
"Everything belongs to us
and yet to no one. This land is your mother. Do you own your mother,
or does she give herself until you stand?
When you walk upon the soil, walk gently. She is not property. She is kin."
That night the boy who tried to hold the earth planted his hands in the dirt and
whispered, "I am yours and you are mine
not as a master, not as a slave but as family."
And for the first time,
he felt the ground answer beneath him, steady and alive.

Verse 3
The Illusion of Ownership

They say,

"This is mine
my land, my lover, my life.".

But what can truly be owned
in a world made of dust and departure?

I have tried to hold things
names, faces, memories
only to watch them slip through the fingers of time
like grains in a desert wind.

Even this body is on loan from the earth.

And still
I love.
Not to possess but to praise.
Not to grip but to give thanks
for what is here now.

Love becomes sacred when you stop calling it yours.
The rose does not bloom for you
it simply blooms.

So let us live like that
offering beauty without needing applause,
walking through this world with open palms
and nothing to steal.

A monk once poured tea into a visitor's cup until it spilled over.
The visitor shouted, "Stop! The cup is full!"
The monk bowed,
"And so is your mind
full of names and opinions. Nothing more can enter."

But what is a cup if not a prison for water?
What is a name if not a fence built around the infinite?

We call a tree "tree," and forget it is a cathedral of wind,
A ladder for birds,
A choir of leaves that clap for the sun.
We call a river "river," and forget it is a vein of the earth,
A mirror for the moon,

A serpent carrying both life and death in its coils.
And when we name each other
enemy, friend, sinner, saint
We trade the living soul for a carved mask.
We mistake the costume for the dancer,
The word for the truth it tries to bind.

The Tao whispers:
"Once you name me, I am not what you name.
Once you claim me, I slip through your hands."

To label is to limit. To define is to divide.
To cling to names is to hold smoke in your fists.

So become like the sky
Vast, nameless, refusing capture. Drink from the cup only when it is empty.
See with eyes that do not cage what they behold.
Then at last, the world will rise up unbroken before you,
Not a list of names,
But a song without

end.

Verse 4
To Label Is to Limit

To name a thing
is to place it in a box
beautiful perhaps,
but still a box.

The moment I call myself
"this" or "that,"
I have clipped my own wings.

Others see me through
windows shaped by their wounds,
by their wonder, by their want.

No one sees the same sky
so how can they see the same me?

I used to chase definitions,
carve my identity in stone.
But stone breaks and I was not made to stay still.
Now I open my hands
and release the label,
like a bird I once kept for the sound of its song.

Let it fly.
Because I am not what I think I am.
Nor what you say I am.
I am
what I am becoming
when I let go.

A fisherman once mended his net by the Galilee shore.
A stranger walked by and said, "Follow me."

He did not ask where. He did not weigh the cost.
He simply stood up, leaving his nets and his name behind.
Some say it was his choice. But was it?
Or was it the sea itself that pulled him?
The tide that had always been rising in his blood?

You did not choose the beating of your heart.
You did not choose the breath that fills your lungs each dawn.
You did not choose the hunger that drives you toward truth,
Nor the thirst that bends you toward love.

The vine does not choose the Gardener.
The clay does not choose the Potter.
The child does not choose the womb in which it is knit. And yet
Each is chosen.

Christ said, "You did not choose me. I chose you."
But his words were not a boast. They were a mirror
Showing that we are always chosen,
Long before our "yes" ever formed on our lips.

Think of the seed buried in earth. It does not choose to crack.
It does not choose the sun that warms it.
And yet, when the time comes, It rises, green and trembling, into the light.

So too with you.
You may spend your life thinking you are the chooser,
The decider, the master of your way but one day you will realize
You were already chosen. By love. By truth.
By the mystery that planted you here.

Chosen without choosing. Called without knowing.
And your only answer is to rise.

Verse 5
Chosen Without Choosing

No, I didn't choose this life
not like a king chooses war
Or a merchant his ship.

But when the time came to weigh it all
The ache, the awe,
the strange miracle of being
One small heartbeat in a galaxy mostly silent

I said: Why not?

We live better than monarchs ever dreamed,
engines with a thousand horses beneath us,
Intelligence shaped in code,
Entertainment conjured with a swipe.

In a world where nothing is forced
Not greatness, not stagnation

Why not live?
Let me be the ordinary, done extraordinarily well.
Let me taste morning rain,
crave bread like a child,
And find meaning in the way someone says my name.

I was not forced. I was not tricked.
I saw the terror and the treasure and said:
So be it. I'll go.

Because to be God is to be human
Where mystery still breathes,
And the future
still
surprises.

006   The Truth You Already Carry (Parable)

They tell of an old sage, Laozi, who came to the city gates.
The guards begged him:
"Write down your wisdom before you leave."
And so he took the brush, wrote the Way on bamboo strips, Then disappeared into the
mountains.

But the truth he wrote was not new. It was not invented that day at the gate.
It was already in the soil, in the rivers, in the sky,
And in the hearts of those who had the eyes to see.

We are all wanderers at that same gate,
Asking for scrolls, for scriptures, for words carved in stone.
But the truth you seek cannot be handed to you.
It is not hidden in temples or locked inside books.

It lives in the marrow of your bones, in the quiet between your thoughts,
In the silence that follows your last question.
Think of the traveler who carries water on his back, Complaining of thirst all the way
Never realizing the jug has been full from the beginning.
Think of the child who searches the house for her mother,
Crying out in every room
While the mother has been holding her hand the whole time.

This is the paradox:
You search for what you already are. You pray for what has never left you. You
hunger for what is already in your mouth.

The sage at the gate only reminded us:
The treasure is not beyond the horizon but buried under your own feet. The path is not
to acquire but to uncover. Not to become,
but to remember.

The truth you already carry is this
You are not apart from the Way.
You are the Way, Walking itself,

Forgetting and remembering in every step.

Verse 6
The Truth You Already Carry
(There Are No Accidents in Nature)

What I teach you is not new.
It has been etched in your DNA
like ancient songs buried in bone.

So why do you chase truth as if it lives outside you?

It is in the trees
not as metaphor but as mirror.

It is in the wind
not as mystery but as memory.

It is in the dirt, in the water, in your breath.
It is in you. It is you.

Love yourself
not as an act of defiance,
but as a return to order.

Because there has never been a wrong time
for a flower to bloom,
nor a wrong sky for rain to fall.

And if nature makes no mistakes,
then you, too, are no accident.

You are not late. You are not broken.

You are simply a symptom of nature
awakening right on time.

007 Soul Within a Soul (Parable)

In a town on a hill with a bell that went BONG,
Lived a boy with a book that was barely a song.

The book was so tiny, it fit in his palm,
Its cover was wrinkled, its pages were calm.

He opened it wide and
oh, what a sight!
A city of voices, all shining with light!
They danced and they played, they worked and they dreamed,
Each one believing they reigned supreme.
But one little person (so tiny, so small),
Whispered, "Perhaps we're not biggest at all...

For look at this speck that I hold in my hand,
It quivers and glitters like grains of the sand!"
Inside that small speck (though it seemed quite absurd),
Lived a whole other people, who never had hear
Of the bigger ones living just over their skies,
Who thought they were largest,
And clever and wise.

And down it went further and deeper and more,
Each soul held a soul in the heart of its core.
Like candles in lanterns, like dolls in a row,
Each world in another, wherever you go.

The boy closed the book and he sat very still,
With the wind on his cheek and the sun on the hill.

And he asked with a whisper, both gentle and true,
"Am I in a story? Am I in one too?"

Verse 7
Soul Within the Soul

The soul is not in the body. That is the ancient mistake
as if forever could be poured into flesh.

No
we are the body, floating in soul.
Suspended in the breath that breathed the stars into being.

The breath is not ours.
It is the pulse of the universe flowing through us,
not for possession but for purpose.
The soul does not grow for power
but for the what's new and exciting.
Not for more but for true self discovery.

It stretches
yes
but not with greed.
Like fire fed just enough, it becomes light, not destruction.

Take too much,
and you lose yourself.
Take too little,
and life breaks you.

But take what is needed
with reverence, with discipline
and even an ordinary body
becomes an unstoppable vessel of precise will.

The forgotten soul was never truly gone.
It is the silence behind your thoughts.
The rhythm in your chest.
The presence that waits for you to remembered
you were never just the body.

Reflection / Notes

Part II The Fire of Becoming
Breathe work: Bellows Breath

Ignite the Flame
"The Breath that Stokes Your Becoming"

How to Practice:
Sit tall, spine long.
Begin rapid breaths through the nose equal inhale and exhale durations (about one second each).VPump the belly like a bellows: in and out. Start with 15 seconds, then rest. Gradually increase to 1 minute, always taking breaks. Do not strain or force. Build gradually.

Prompt: With each breath, imagine lighting the furnace within.
You're not burning out you're burning through.
Evolution takes heat. Be the fire, not the ash.

Breath Pattern: Rapid inhale/exhale through nose equal durations
Start with 15 seconds → Rest → Gradually increase up to 1 minute
Repeat in sets with breaks

This is an energizing breath that stokes inner fire. Your body may heat up. Eyes may water. Mind may race. Good. That's your soul waking up.
Use this breath before decision making, workouts, or moments when you must rise. It's for momentum not meditation. But always listen to your body. Don't use this breath if you're dizzy, anxious, or pregnant.
Honor your edge. This is evolution breath it burns old skin and makes way for the new.

What to Let Go:
The shame that says change means betrayal.
The comfort of staying small.
The voices that mock your hunger.

What to Hold On To:
 Your divine right to transform. The fire in your belly.
The courage to burn what no longer fits.
Reflection: This is becoming. Not escaping evolving.

008 Becoming Is My Birthright (Parable)

An elder sat by the fire, the night stretched wide and ancient around them.
The stars were sharp above, cold and countless,
While the flames below cracked and twisted,
shadows leaping against the trees like restless spirits.
Beside him, his grandchild fidgeted.

Too young to name the ache in his chest.
Too restless to sit still while the silence of the forest pressed down.
The elder took a stick and stirred the fire. Two shapes rose in the smoke
one black as ash, its eyes glinting with hunger,
The other pale and steady, its breath slow, its fur like woven mist.

"These two dwell in every heart,"
the elder said. "One is the beast of greed, born from fear, Always gnawing, never full.
The other is the wolf of stillness, it's strength quiet, it's path sure. Together, they circle
one another, claws scratching across the soul."

The child leaned closer, watching the shadows fight in the firelight.
The snarling wolf lunged, snapping sparks into the air,
While the calm wolf only held its ground, Unmoved, as if it drew its strength not from
fighting but from belonging to the night itself.

"Which one wins, Grandfather?"
the child whispered, voice breaking like a twig in the dark.
The elder's eyes, lit by flame, carried both fury and peace,
Both hunger and contentment.

And he said,
"Neither wins, unless you choose. For the fire burns only what is fed. So ask yourself
Will you feed the beast that devours, Or the one that endures?"

The night stretched on and the boy felt the wolves stir inside him
Not as strangers but as companions. He understood then that both lived within,
And his life would be nothing less than the story. Of which fire he chose to keep
alive.

Verse 8
Becoming Is My Birthright

I do not owe the world consistency.
Only sincerity.

Let them say,
"You've changed."
Let them whisper,
"You're not the same."

Of course I am not the same. What is a river that refuses to move?

Stagnant. Sick. Forgotten.

I am the flood, the drought, the gentle stream and the roaring fall.
I have outgrown the self I wore last season.
And I will outgrow this one too.

Every truth I hold is but a stepping stone
not a throne.

Becoming is my birthright.
Changing is my prayer.
Contradiction is my teacher.

So do not cage me in your past memory.
I will disappoint it beautifully.

Because I was not made to be known.
I was made to be discovered

Again,
and again and again

009   The Clay of Becoming (Parable)

They say Prometheus shaped the first of us from clay.
Kneeling at the riverbank, his hands sank into the mud and with every pinch and
press,
he tried to mirror the divine but the clay cracked.
It dried too quickly or collapsed in his palms like wet sand.

It was never perfect
never smooth. So he kept shaping, again and again,
not to reach an end but to stay faithful to the act of forming.
When the fire of heaven was stolen to animate the figures,
The gods cursed him for daring to kindle mortals with their flame.
But Prometheus only smiled, for he knew

The true gift wasn't the fire at all
It was the clay.
The chance to begin, to collapse, to reshape,
And to become. And so we inherit that same mud,
That same stubborn earth that refuses to hold its form for long.
Our lives crumble, our identities crack,

And yet
still
we press the fragments back together,
Always half finished, always in motion.
To be human is to be sculptor and sculpture at once.

Our hands shaping, our hearts softening,
Our failures folding back into the mix.

We are not here to harden into statues,
But to remain clay, alive to the touch,

Always ready to be remade.

Verse 9
The Clay of Becoming

I am not finished.

And I pray I never will be.

Because the moment I call myself complete,
I've mistaken the sculpture for the sculptor.
Mistaken the fire for the ash.

They ask me who I am,
but I am still wet clay
spinning on the wheel of breathe,
of heartbreak,
of awe.

Every name I've worn has been both shelter and trap.
Every truth I've clung to has cracked,
only to let light in.

So I speak now with loosened tongue,
walk now with softened steps,
hold now with open palms.

For the wise
do not harden into form
they become water.

And even water leaves room for more

sky.

010   The Wisdom of the Wound (Parable)

A disciple once asked a teacher,
"Why must suffering touch us? If God is love, why does pain strike so deep?"

The teacher lifted his sleeve and revealed a scar across his arm.
"See this wound? When it was fresh,
it burned and bled. I hated it. I wanted it gone. But now it has healed,
and though the skin is never the same, it is stronger where it tore.
The scar is a map, reminding me I survived."

He told a story:
when Christ's hands were pierced,
the world thought it was defeat.
But from those wounds poured a love so fierce it refused to vanish.
By his wounds, the suffering of others was seen, remembered,
and carried. Pain, instead of ending the story,
became the door through which compassion walked.

So it is with us.
To live unbroken is to remain shallow.
To be cracked is to know depth. A person who has never been wounded
cannot sit beside the grieving and understand their silence.
But the one who has bled can recognize another's trembling hands
and whisper,
"I know."

The wisdom of the wound is this:
what hurts us most has the power to open us most.

Pain hollows us, yes
but it hollows us into vessels wide enough to hold
Love.

Verse 10
The Wisdom of the Wound

The wound
does not ask for shame
only understanding.

Pain is not punishment.

It is a lantern
lit by the fire of awareness.
Where it hurts is where the lesson waits.

I have run from my ache,
buried it beneath distraction,
but it waits patiently
until I am quiet enough to listen.

The wound is a doorway.
Not a dead end.
It breaks me open only to show me what I've been carrying for too long.

A sorrow inherited;
A belief unchallenged; A fear misunderstood.

When I stop resisting, I see clearly:
This wound was not meant to close too quickly.

It was meant to speak.
And when it does,
may I not silence it
but bow

There was once a forest wounded by fire.
Its trees stood blackened and hollow, the ground scarred, the rivers choked with ash.
The people who lived nearby argued over what should be done.
Some demanded to clear the ruin and plant quickly, others wanted to build houses
where the trees had fallen and others still walked away, calling the forest dead.

But the elders said nothing.
They did not touch the land, nor did they force it to rise before its time.
They waited. And in the waiting, a strange thing happened. The rains returned.

The rivers carved new paths.
Tiny shoots of green pierced through the charred soil, delicate yet unashamed. Birds
began to circle overhead, their songs testing the silence.
Then one day, a stag walked softly between the blackened trunks,
not as an intruder but as a herald.

The forest, by its own wisdom, had chosen to heal.
The elders gathered the children and pointed:
"See this? Not all things are mended by our hands. Some wounds close only in
stillness. Some pains bloom only when left alone."

The children looked closer. They saw moss creeping up burned bark,
covering scars without erasing them. They saw fallen logs now hosting mushrooms,
feeding life through their decay.
They saw that silence itself was medicine
the absence of interference allowing the earth to remember its own strength.

And so the forest became their teacher.
It told them that grief, too, is such a wound. If you pick at it, it bleeds. If you
command it, it resists. But if you honor it with time and space, it roots itself into
wisdom.

Generations later, when new flames rose elsewhere, the story was told again: of the
forest that healed because it was left in peace,
and of the people who learned that to love something broken is sometimes to leave it
untouched.

Verse 11
How to Heal the Heart

Like any wound
clean it.
Let tears fall, if they come. Do not be ashamed. Tears are holy water.

They draw out what festers when silence can't hold it alone.
Feel it fully.

Let the ache pass through like a traveler.
But do not invite it to stay.
Do not pour tea for the past.

Do not feed the pain with stories. Do not braid it into identity.

"A wound fed by memory becomes a shrine to suffering."

Place your hand over it. Not to fix
but to bless.

Your hand is a prayer. Your stillness, a cleansing.
Apply truth like ointment: It happened. It hurt. It shaped you but it is not you.

Then
cover it.

Not to hide but to shield while it learns the quiet art of becoming whole.
Like a seed beneath soil, healing does not beg to be seen.

And most of all
stop touching it. Stop checking if it still hurts.
The Tao flows where the hand withdraws. The seeker spins until pain becomes wind.

The student breathes
and lets it go freely.

Healing isn't loud. It arrives in stillness. When you finally stop chasing it
and trust it.

012   To Be the Fire Without Burning (Parable)

In the ancient temple of the fire,
the priests tended a flame said to be eternal.
No wind nor storm could extinguish it,
for it was fed by careful hands and reverent silence.
A young seeker once asked the high priest,
"Why worship fire? Is it not dangerous, a thing that consumes?"

The priest smiled and gestured to the flame.
"Look closer. The fire devours, yes
but only what is given to it.
It does not leap from the altar to scorch the world. It waits, steady, pure."

The seeker bowed.
"And what does this teach me of my own heart?"
"That you too may burn without burning,"

the priest replied.
"To carry passion without destroying, to shine without scorching those near you.
Anger unleashed is wildfire,
but discipline makes it a hearth.
Desire untamed consumes but guided it gives warmth and light."

The seeker stayed through the night,
watching the flame.
He saw in its dance both hunger and restraint,
both power and peace.

And when dawn came, he whispered to himself:
"I too must become a fire tended
not raging, not hidden but steady. A light to warm, not a blaze to wound."

For to be human is not to extinguish the flame within,
But to learn how to burn without burning.

Verse 12
The Fire That Does Not Burn

I met God once
in the hollow of my chest

not in thunder
but in a whisper.
Not a man with a beard,
not a judge on a throne but a warmth
that did not demand to be named.

It did not ask for prayer.
Only presence.
In that silence, I understood:
the sacred is not far,
it is folded in every overlooked moment.

The touch of water.
The ache of longing.
The sound of your own name
when whispered with love.

I no longer seek heaven as a place above
I find it in the kindness of strangers,
in tears not hidden, in laughter without masks.

This fire does not burn. It illuminates.

And I
I am learning to be light.

013   Imperfectly Perfect (Parable)

A Zen master once held up a bowl before his students.
It was cracked, its broken edges stitched with rivers of gold.

"Is this bowl broken?" he asked.
One student said, "Yes, master. The cracks prove its failure."

Another said, "No, master. It still holds tea."

But the master only smiled and poured steaming tea into the veins of gold,
letting the fragrance rise.

"You see," he said,
"perfection is not the absence of flaw,
but the embrace of it. This bowl is more whole now than before, for it tells its story
honestly. Its breaking was not the end
it was the beginning of truth."

The students stared, their eyes caught in the shimmer of the seams.
One thought of a scar across his cheek, another of grief hidden under silence. Some
bowed in shame, for they had tried so hard to keep their lives unbroken. Others wept
openly, realizing their wounds had always been their most human prayers.

The master continued:
"When you break, do not seek to erase the breaking. Do not grind yourself to dust,
pretending to be untouched. Instead, mend yourself with gold
the gold of patience, the gold of compassion, the gold of love. Let others see your
scars. They are the maps of where you have been,
and the proof that you still carry the strength to hold."

He passed the bowl to the youngest student,
who trembled as she received it.
For the first time, she understood that her own fractures
Were not evidence of weakness,
but invitations to beauty. And so the cracked bowl moved from hand to hand, a silent
scripture, more eloquent than any words
Reminding each that imperfection is not the opposite of beauty,
But the very doorway into it.

Verse 13 Imperfectly Perfect
(The Sacred Role of Emotion)

They told me emotions were bad
That showing them meant you had weakness

That truth lives only in stillness.
But who are we without our storms?
What is fire without its burn?

Even the tear has purpose. Even anger teaches. Even sorrow is a sculptor,

Chiseling the heart into something wide enough to hold compassion.

No emotion is wrong
They may not be truth but they lead to it.

Each one, a torch in the tunnel.

Grief says: You loved.
Jealousy whispers: You care.
Fear warns: You're growing.
And joy? It reminds: You are still alive.

The universe does not waste creation.
It made the wolf and the lamb
And called both sacred.

So let us stop killing parts of ourselves
To appear holy.
Let us integrate the whole storm,

And call it sky.

A weary musician once approached the Buddha, his guitar slung across his back. His face was lined with the years of chasing songs that never seemed finished.

He bowed and asked, "Master, how do I live without breaking myself? How do I find balance?" The Buddha motioned to the guitar. "Play," he said.
The musician plucked a string so tightly wound that it snapped with a sharp cry, startling even the birds. The Buddha nodded gently.
"And what happens when the string is stretched too tight?"
"It breaks," the musician answered. "Then loosen it."
The man obeyed, letting the string fall slack.
He plucked it again but no sound came, only a dull lifeless vibration.
"And what happens when the string is too loose?" the Buddha asked. "It will not sing." The Buddha looked at him, eyes soft as dawn.
"Then balance is not found in the extremes but in the tuning. Not too tight, not too loose. Only in the middle will the string give its song."
The musician adjusted the string carefully, plucked it and the air filled with a clear and living note. He closed his eyes as the sound lingered, as if time itself bowed to listen.
"Life is this way," the Buddha continued.
"When you are stretched with ambition beyond your strength, you will break. When you are slack with despair or idleness, you will wither. But when you walk the middle path, when you learn the art of tension balanced with rest, discipline softened with mercy
your life becomes music."
The musician wept, for he saw his own soul as the instrument. He had lived years either pulling too hard or letting go too much, never hearing the simple beauty of his own note. Now, for the first time, he understood:
balance was not a compromise but the tuning of existence.
And so he played, each string adjusted with care, until the song rose into the evening air. Villagers gathered, drawn by the sound.
They heard in his melody a teaching no sermon could carry that joy is not found at the edges but in the middle of all things, where harmony waits to be struck.
The Buddha closed his eyes and listened, smiling. For truth had been made into music and music into truth.

Verse 14
The Middle of All Things (A verse on sacred balance)

What should I let go of ego, desire, fear, or love?
These are the mistakes of men and to what end.
Where to draw the fine line of taking things too far?
As if things we know are wrong are justified due to our laziness.
We always do too much or too little to what only benefits us only!
Leaving the one who is supposed to learn the lesson,
Learn nothing while we feed our ego.

So maybe now, let's become more humble
Instead of jumping into conclusions and giving advice, let's go to understand

For the reed does not curse the wind. It bends and thus, it sings.
The fire does not shame its hunger
It warms, because it knows its place. Even the desert, vast and merciless,
Hides water beneath
Not to deny it,

But to teach the seeker to thirst with discipline. Do not kill the ego. Refine it.
Let it be the servant, not the king.
Do not silence fear. Understand it.

It guards the threshold between habit and transformation.
Even Love, the wildest of winds must learn the weight of roots,
Or it will topple the tree instead of growing it.

And what of happiness?
It comes not from chasing but from being
A side effect of inner harmony and the dance with life,
Not the prize of outer effort.
Walk not left, not right.

Not above, not below.
But the middle of all things
Where silence speaks and stillness my sanctuary

A child was once learning to walk in a small courtyard. She clung to the wall at first, shuffling sideways, then, bold with new courage, she let go. For three steps she was a queen, ruling the earth with her stride. On the fourth, she tumbled face first into the dust. She cried, not from pain but from betrayal, the ground had seemed her enemy. But when her mother lifted her and set her back down, the child discovered that falling had taught her balance in a way standing never could.

So it has always been. Adam reached for the fruit and fell, yet in falling he learned the burden of choice. Icarus spread his wings too wide and fell, yet in falling the sky itself was remembered in men's stories.
Kingdoms rise and fall, lovers fall into and out of each other, trees shed their leaves into death each autumn, yet it is in the descent that renewal waits.
One evening, an old monk spoke to his students after watching one of them fail at a chant again and again. The young man's voice cracked, his pride cracked harder.
"Master," he said bitterly, "why does heaven allow us to stumble so?"
The monk answered by taking the boy's clay cup and dashing it to the stone floor. It shattered. Silence swallowed the room. Then the master swept up the pieces, ground them with water and set the clay to dry. "Tomorrow," he said, "we will make a stronger cup. Do you see now? Heaven does not humiliate. Heaven remakes."

The lesson is this: the fall is not a curse but a curriculum. Without the stumble, there is no balance. Without the fracture, there is no mending. Without loss, no hunger for what is lasting. The dust we fear is the very dust from which we rise, again and again. Even the earth itself fell, from fire into stone, from chaos into order, from molten rivers into rivers of water. And in each collapse, something greater took shape. So when you fall, do not call yourself broken. Call yourself taught. For the ground is not your enemy, it is your teacher, waiting with open arms

Verse 15
The Fall That Teaches

They warned me of the fall
as if falling were failure,
as if descent were death.

But I found more sky beneath me
than I ever saw above.
It is not the falling that breaks you,
it is the refusal to fall.
To cling to the ledge with bleeding fingers
is the true suffering.

The fall teaches what the summit never could:
that you are not the height you reach,
but the ground you learn to rise from.

We speak of falling as if it were foolish,
but perhaps it is the only way
to land in something real.

To fall is to return
to humility, to breath, to Earth.

And when you rise again, you do not rise alone.
You rise with knowing, with softened pride,
with wings forged not from victory but from surrender.

So fall.
Let it break what must be broken.
Let it teach you what only the fall can know.

Reflection / Notes

Part III   The Sacred Exit
Breathe work: Box Breathing

Exit with Honor
"The Breath of Boundaries and Balance"

How to Practice:
Inhale for 4 counts. Hold at the top for 4. Exhale for 4.
Hold at the bottom for 4. Repeat this steady square. No rush.

Prompt:
Trace a glowing square in your mind. Each corner lights with breath.
With every box, you build a doorway   not to escape but to choose.
This is your temple of clarity.

Breath Pattern:
Inhale (4) → Hold (4) → Exhale (4) → Hold (4)
Repeat slowly for 2 5 minutes
This breath builds emotional steadiness and disciplined release.

Each phase is a wall of protection around your stillness.
Visualize a glowing square each side built from your breath.
Use this breath when emotions threaten your clarity.
Or when you're stepping away from something heavy.
This is exit not with bitterness but with mastery.

What to Let Go:
The fear of being alone after walking away.
The belief that peace requires permission.
The debt of being understood.

What to Hold On To:
Your intuition. The silence that honors goodbye.
The right to leave something without guilt.

Reflection:
This is balance. Not numbness   discernment.
Exit with honor.

A young monk once asked his master,
"How can love be both free and bound?
How can it soar like a bird yet still stay rooted like a tree?"

The master led him to a river.
"Do you see this water? If it spills across the land, it floods and destroys.
But when given banks, it becomes the river of life
feeding villages, turning wheels, quenching thirst.
Love is the same. Without discipline, it drowns. With discipline, it nourishes."

The monk watched the current rush between its edges,
wild yet guided. He thought of his own heart
how it longed to pour out endlessly, yet often left chaos behind.

The master spoke again:
"Love without discipline is desire dressed as freedom.
It takes more than it gives. But disciplined love is freedom in its truest form. It bends,
it flows, it moves with patience, yet it always knows where it is going. The river does
not fear its banks it sings because of them."

The monk lowered his eyes.
He remembered the pain of clinging too tightly and the shame of giving himself too
loosely. He realized that love was not about having no boundaries,
nor about building walls. It was about learning to honor
the banks that let love flow into eternity.

That night, he returned to the river alone. He dipped his hand into its water and
whispered,
"Let me be a river, not a flood.
Let me learn to love with discipline, so that my love may endure."

And the current, endless and steady, carried his prayer away
toward the sea that holds all rivers and the

Love that requires no chains
because it already knows the way.

Verse 16
Love With Discipline

Love is not the fire alone
it is the hand that tends it. Not passion without pause but devotion shaped by
intention.

For what is love without discipline? A river without banks
spilling, flooding, consuming until nothing remains. But love with discipline?

It is the garden in the desert,
watered not by impulse but by commitment.
To love someone is to study their seasons,
to endure the winters,
to plant even when the soil feels dry.

It is not to possess but to protect.

Not to demand but to understand
that change is not betrayal,
and growth is not abandonment.

Love does not just feel.

It learns.
Like the mystic bowing daily,
like the student sweeping the floor
repetition becomes reverence.

Discipline becomes devotion.
And love,
no longer a fleeting ache,
becomes a path walked in bare feet,
day by sacred day.

A father once planted a small fig tree
in the corner of his garden.
He gave it rich soil, water and shade and every morning
he whispered blessings into its leaves.

The tree grew tall but soon its branches
leaned dangerously, heavy with fruit.
The father placed a wooden stake beside it,
tying the trunk gently so it would not snap under its own weight.

One of his neighbors mocked him:
"If you love the tree,
let it grow as it wishes. Why bind it?"

The father answered,
"I do not bind it to harm it. I guide it,
so it may stand long after I am gone.
Love without direction is not love
it is neglect."

Years passed and storms came.
The wind shook every tree in the garden and many fell.
Yet the fig tree stood firm, bearing fruit season after season.

The father, now old, rested beneath
its shade and said to his grandson:
"Love is unconditional in its roots
always giving, always patient.
But its branches need conditions, guidance,
and measure, lest they break too soon.
To love unconditionally is to give life.
To love conditionally is to teach it how to endure."

And so the boy understood that love
is both freedom and form,
wildness and wisdom,
unconditional in spirit but conditional in practice

like a tree tied not to weaken it but to keep it growing strong.

Verse 17
Becoming

They told me:
"Love without condition."

But what is a love
that asks for nothing?

That receives betrayal, silence, or harm
and still calls it holy?

Even the earth sets conditions:

the seed must crack, the sun must rise, the rain must come.

So I say:
Let love be like breath
offered freely but with rhythm.

Let it be unconditional in presence
but conditional in practice.
Unconditional in hope,
but conditional in how we are treated.

For boundaries are not cages
they are prayers with shape.

And I, too, am sacred ground.
I will not beg to be watered by a careless hand.

So let me love like the wise river:

flowing where it can,
turning when it must,
and always knowing
where not to go.

A student came to a master,
heart swollen with knowledge.
He had read every scroll, memorized every verse,
and filled his tongue with answers before questions even arrived.

The master welcomed him,
and without a word, set a cup between them.
He poured tea until the cup filled, then kept pouring.
The tea spilled over, soaking the table,
dripping to the earth below.
Still he poured.

The student could no longer contain himself.
"Master, the cup is full
it can take no more!"

The master stopped at last and looked at him with eyes that had seen the same mistake
a thousand times.
"Like this cup, you are full.
Full of words, full of certainty, full of yourself.
How can truth enter you when there is no space left?"

The student stared at the overflowing cup. He wanted to protest,
but the silence pressed against him like the weight of the sky.
He saw the puddle spreading, carrying steam across the floor,
sinking into the cracks of stone.

For the first time in his life,
he swallowed his reply instead of speaking it.
He breathed and in that pause,
a small emptiness appeared inside him
wide enough for a seed of wisdom to fall through.

And the master smiled,
for he knew:

until the student could become empty,
he would never taste what is full.

Verse 18
Love, The Student

I do not want to be a master of love.
Masters stop learning.
I want to be its student. Always.

Love is not a subject to conquer
it is a mystery to sit with.

A mirror
I must face again and again,
only to see a new version
of myself reflected back.

I do not teach love.
I learn it with every conversation.
I learn it when someone leaves.
I learn it when I'm wrong.

I learn it
when I love someone who can't love me back
and still wish them well.

Love makes me humble.
Because every person I love
will become a different person tomorrow.

And if I do not stay a student
I will miss the lesson they've become.

So teach me, Love.
Let me take notes in your classroom of
pain, of joy, of waiting.

Let me fail tests and learn again.
Because I do not want the kind of love that knows.
I want the kind of love that asks.
And keeps asking.

019 Love Defined (Parable)

A scholar once asked a sage, "Tell me plainly
what is love? I have studied the scriptures of every faith,
yet the answer remains tangled in riddles."

The sage held up a lamp and said, "This flame is love. It warms the room,
it gives light to see, yet if you grasp it with your bare
hand it will burn you."

The scholar frowned. "So love is dangerous?"

The sage shook his head.
"No. Love is fire itself; it cannot be safe; it cannot be tamed
But it can be honored. Fire does not exist to be locked in a box,
nor does love exist to be controlled. It is meant to move, to dance, to transform."

Still unsatisfied, the scholar pressed on.
"But how do I know if the fire I hold is truly love and not just desire dressed in
disguise?"

The sage poured oil into the lamp and replied:
"Desire burns quickly, consuming all until nothing remains.
Love burns steadily, feeding not on what it takes but on what it gives.
Desire says, 'Stay with me so I am not empty.'
Love says, 'Take what I have, even if you leave.'"

The scholar was quiet, watching the flame.
He thought of the people he had claimed to love, how often he had wanted them to fill
his loneliness rather than share their freedom.

The sage continued:
"To define love is to fail it, for words are walls
and love is the wind. But if you must name it, call it this
love is the fire that does not end, the light that does not blind,
the warmth that does not demand.
It is the only wealth that increases the more it is given away."
The scholar bowed low, tears glinting in the lamp's glow.
He realized then that love could never be captured in a page or formula.
It could only be lived and in living, known.

Verse 19
Love Defined

Love for Me:

"To become the best version of yourself for someone else"

Not to fill a void
but to honor the gift of presence.

Not because you lack but because something sacred in them
calls forth what's buried in you.
Other paths may ask you to erase, to vanish the self,
to dissolve into silence or surrender to some higher mold.

But my love is not disappearance.
It is emergence.

It is not to deny who I am
but to become more of it,
with reverence.

I do not burn the ego to ash,
I temper it in the fire of relationship,
until it shines like gold.

I do not worship sacrifice
I bow to becoming.

And Love,
Love is not sugar,
Sweetness alone spoils the soul.
Even honey must be held in balance

So I love
with sharp truth and soft hands,
with honest mirrors and opened doors.

Not to complete,
not to fix
but to stand beside and become.

020   The Fire and the Flower (Parable)

A young monk once asked his teacher,
"Why does love feel like both a blessing and a curse?
One moment it is a garden, the next it is a wildfire."

The teacher led him to the monastery courtyard
where two things grew side by side: a wild flame flickering in a clay lamp and a
single lotus rising from the pond.

"Look closely," the teacher said.
"The fire gives warmth and light but if left unguarded it will consume the lamp itself.
The flower gives fragrance and beauty but if plucked too quickly it will wither before
its time."

The monk studied them. "So fire is passion and the flower is tenderness?"

The teacher nodded. "Yes. To love is to hold both
the fire and the flower. If you cling only to the fire, you will burn those you love. If
you cling only to the flower, you will smother it with your need to possess. But when
you honor both, you create balance. Fire protects the flower through the night and the
flower teaches the fire where to rest."

The monk sat in silence, listening to the crackle of the flame and the soft sway of
petals in the wind. He thought of those he had loved
how often he had burned them with intensity or crushed them with fear of losing
them.

The teacher placed the lotus into the monk's hands,
then held the lamp near enough for its warmth to brush his skin
without burning.

"Love is not one or the other. It is the dance of opposites,
the unity of tenderness and power, the patience to let a
flower bloom and the courage to carry fire without fear.
It is not fragile, nor is it wild
it is both and more."

And from that day, whenever the monk prayed,
he kept a lamp and a flower beside him. Not as idols but as reminders
that true love is always fire and flower,
never one without the other.

Verse 20
"The Fire and the Flower"

A man once stood before the Master,
his voice sharp,
his words soaked in poison.
He insulted him again and again,
waiting for anger to rise.

But the Master only smiled and asked:
"If you offer a gift and it is not accepted
to whom does it belong?"

The man replied,
"To the giver."

"Then so it is with your anger,"
said the Master.
"You bring me fire but I carry no fuel.
You offer me a wound but I do not open."

So too, with love. If you give it and it is not received,
it remains in your hands.

That is not failure
only truth.

Love must be planted to grow.
Anger must be met to burn.
Even water drowns when it knows no shore.
Even passion destroys when it has no direction.

Balance is not the absence of emotion
but the wisdom to carry, release, or let rest.
And if we must walk through this life,
let us carry what nourishes.

Let the flames die in the hands that clutch them.
Let love be poured
only where it may bloom.

A seeker once approached a sage with a heavy question:
"Should I love myself without condition or
should I discipline myself with condition?
If I accept myself too freely, I grow lazy.
If I discipline myself too harshly, I grow bitter. Which path is true?"

The sage smiled and led the seeker to a riverbank.
The water rushed swiftly, wild and free,
yet it never overflowed its bed of stone.

"Look at the river," the sage said.
"It flows without condition
it does not ask permission to be water
but its strength is guided by the banks. Without the stones,
the river would flood and destroy. Without the water,
the stones would lie lifeless and dry.
Together, they make life possible."

The seeker frowned. "So I must be both the water and the stone?"

"Exactly," the sage said.
"Love yourself as unconditionally as the water flows.
Accept your nature, your essence, without shame.
But also set the conditions of discipline,
as firm as the stones, so your energy is not wasted.
To love unconditionally without discipline is chaos.
To live conditionally without love is prison.
The way is to unite both."

The seeker knelt, letting the river wash over his hands.
He saw how the water shaped the stones smooth,
and how the stones kept the water alive in its path.
For the first time, he felt that self love was not indulgence,
nor was discipline punishment
it was the marriage of the two.

"Become unconditionally, conditionally you,"
the sage whispered.
"Be the river and the banks. Flow freely but know where you belong."

Verse 21
Becoming Unconditionally, Conditionally You

There is a beauty in limits
like a riverbank shaping the wild water.

To become
unconditionally,
conditionally you
is to honor both your essence and your edges.

Not a surrender to chaos,
nor a rigid fence to hold it all in
but a dance
between grace and ground.

You are not meant to be boundless
if it means being lost.
You are meant to be whole
and wholeness requires form,
as much as it invites freedom.

Let the world see you
but not all of you,
not always.

Privacy is not shame.
Boundaries are not betrayal.

They are the soil
where your soul can root.

So be you.
Wildly. Wisely.

With just enough door left open
for the right ones to knock.

Reflection / Notes

Part IV   What Love Remembers
Breathe work: Oceanic Wave Breath

Tide of Memory
"The Breath of Holding Without Drowning"

How to Practice:
Inhale slowly through the nose   belly → ribs → chest.
Exhale with a soft oceanic "haaah" through mouth or nose.
Each breath cycle lasts about 10 12 seconds. Let it flow.
No force. Let your breath move like a tide.

Prompt:
With each wave, memory returns or fades. Grief rides in but so does grace. The ocean
never forces   it just keeps coming back.

Breath Pattern:
Slow, wave like Inhale → Slow Exhale (10 12 sec total)
Repeat gently for 3 5 minutes
Imagine being cradled by water.
This breath heals grief, heartbreak and old tenderness.

It holds space without drowning you.
Let the breath carry memories like driftwood
some float away, some stay.
Practice when remembering love, or when you miss who you were.

What to Let Go:
The belief that love must always hurt.
The fear that you're hard to love.
The armor that kept you from receiving.

What to Hold On To:
The memory of being held once, even in a dream. The ache that proves you cared.

The love still moving beneath the rubble.

Reflection:
This is remembering. Not nostalgia

                              truth.

A potter sat at his wheel, the earth damp between his fingers.
From formless clay, he drew up walls,
shaping a vessel round and hollow.
When the sun dried it and the fire kissed it, it hardened
fragile, yet enduring. He held it up to the light.

"Empty,"
said the student beside him.
"Broken waiting to happen."
The potter smiled.
"This vessel is not weakness. It was born to be hollow,
for its strength is not in what it is but in what it can hold."

He filled it with water, poured grain into it, caught fire within its belly until it glowed.
Its purpose was not diminished by its emptiness
it was defined by it.

One day, a crack split its side.
The student gasped but the potter only nodded.

"Clay remembers the river it came from.
When it breaks, it does not fail
it returns."
He laid the shards gently in the earth,
where rain softened them back to mud.
And again, he began to knead. The vessel's life was never wasted.

In holding, it served. In breaking, it returned.

Its circle was the circle of all things:
birth from dust, fire of transformation, fracture and return.

So too are we.
Fragile vessels, lit with fire, broken and reformed,
carried back to the earth, shaped once more by unseen hands.

And if you fear the cracking of your own walls,
Remember:
even in pieces, clay remembers the river.
And the river remembers you.

Verse 22
The Quiet Rebellion

I used to think
wisdom was loud
a thunderclap of knowing,
a sword
slicing through doubt.

But the wise I met
spoke with their eyes
and listened with their hands.

They built no empires.
They conquered no minds.
They taught by sitting still
as the world spun around them.

In their silence,
I heard everything.

Not the silence of avoidance
but the silence that waits
until truth arrives
barefoot and unannounced.

So I stopped raising my voice
to prove I had one.

I rebelled gently
by being kind, by staying present,
by no longer needing to win.

The world changes
not with noise but with stillness
that refuses to be moved.

A young monk once complained to his teacher:
"Master, I am trapped inside myself.
My thoughts chase me like hounds, my emotions rise like storms,
and no matter where I go, I cannot escape them."

The teacher led him outside,
where the sky stretched endless above the mountains. "Look up,"
he said. "I see clouds, Master," the monk replied.
"Some are dark, some are bright. They move,
but they never stop coming." The teacher nodded. "And yet
are you the clouds?"

The monk hesitated.
"No. I am... the one who sees them."

"Then be the sky,"
said the teacher.
"The sky holds every cloud but is never stained by them.
It welcomes thunder and lightning but remains vast,
untouched, unbroken. Become that sky and you will see
thoughts and feelings will come and go but
they will no longer own you."

The monk stood in silence, his chest loosening for the first time.
He began to breathe as if he had been holding his breath for years.

He watched the clouds drift,
and in their movement he saw his own anger, his grief, his longings
passing, always passing.

That night he sat beneath the open heavens,
letting storms roll through his mind without fear.
He realized that freedom was not about chasing away clouds,
but about remembering that he was never the clouds at all.

And from then on, when others asked him the secret of peace,
he would point to the sky and say:
"Do not fight the weather inside you. Become the sky that holds it."

Verse 23
Becoming the Sky

The mind is a storm but I
I am the sky.

Thoughts rise like dust devils,
regret crashes like thunder,
desire burns like desert sun
but none of these are me.

I am the witness
behind the whirlwind.
The silence that watches without clinging.

They taught me to chase
success, pleasure, identity
but what if peace isn't in pursuit,
but in presence?

The moon does not try to shine.
It reflects.
The tree does not hurry to grow.
It becomes.

So I return to breath.
One inhale, one exhale,
a bow to the moment.

Let them
call me lost
I am simply
no longer
running.

024　The Garden Beyond the Gates (Parable)

There was once a traveler who came upon a great walled garden.
Its gates were heavy iron, shut tight,
with carvings of angels and flames warning any who might approach.

Many people stood outside, peering in through the bars,
longing for what lay within.

Some wept, saying,
"If only we were worthy, perhaps we could enter."
Others shouted prayers at the gate, hoping the keeper inside might hear.
A few tried to climb the walls, only to fall back bruised and broken.

The traveler, however, noticed something strange:
vines spilled freely from within,
carrying blossoms and fruit to the very roadside where he stood.
Birds flew in and out unhindered, singing songs from inside the walls.
The fragrance of the garden filled the air, as if the gates had no power to contain it.

He turned to those waiting and said,
"Why do you beg at the gate when the garden has already spilled into your hands? Do
you not see? You are already standing within its reach."

But they shook their heads. "No," they insisted,
"the true garden is behind the walls."

So the traveler walked on, gathering fruit from the vines that had crossed into the
open world. And with every step, he realized
the garden had never been a place locked away.

The gate was only an illusion, a story told to make people forget the soil beneath their
feet.

When he looked back one last time,
he saw that the gate was not iron at all
it was only fear, painted to look solid.

And beyond fear,
the garden stretched everywhere.

Verse 24
The Garden Beyond the Gate

They told me peace
was past the gate
guarded by time,
earned by toil.

So I wandered.
Through deserts of ambition,
valleys of lovers
who forgot their own names,
mountains carved from my father's
expectations.

And yet, the gate never came.
Until one day, barefoot and tired,

I sat beside a small flower growing
through a crack in the stone.
It did not ask to be seen.
It did not strive to be more.

It just was.
And in its quiet blooming,

I heard a voice
older than scripture say:

"The garden you seek is not beyond the gate.
The gate is your wanting.
The garden is where you stop searching."

So I stayed.

Not because I arrived,

but because I forgot where I was going.

A shaman once asked his apprentices to walk the fields
and return with a single gift from the earth.
One brought back a stone, smooth and heavy, shaped by centuries of rivers.
Another brought a stalk of wheat, golden and bending, full with the promise of bread.
A third returned with a bird's feather, delicate and light as a whisper.
But the last returned with empty hands, saying,
"The earth has already given me air to breathe, water to drink and a body to walk
with. What more could I take?"
The shaman lifted the stone.
"This is the strength of the earth."
He raised the wheat. "This is the abundance of the earth."
He turned the feather. "This is the freedom of the earth."
But when he looked at the apprentice with empty hands, his eyes softened.
"This is gratitude not the search for more but the recognition of enough. You honor
the earth not by what you gather but by the way you see."
The apprentices fell silent,
realizing that their gifts were only symbols.
Yet the one who brought nothing had brought everything
awareness, presence, reverence.
And so the shaman taught them that gratitude is not a word spoken before meals, nor
a prayer whispered in need. It is a vow kept with every breath, a faithfulness that does
not wander after the illusion of more.
Gratitude is how we stay faithful to life,
and how life stays faithful to us.

Verse 25
Gratitude is How We Stay Faithful

To be grateful is not to be naive.

It is to see clearly and still say thank you.
It is how the monk smiles with an empty bowl.

How the wanderer sleeps
beneath the stars without a roof
not because he has nothing
but because he knows
nothing was ever his.

Gratitude is not weakness.
It is the fiercest kind of faith.
It does not ask for more.
It recognizes the miracle of what already is.

To say "this is enough"
is not to settle
it is to bow.

Because the thirst that has no end
turns kings into beggars.

But the one who drinks with reverence
and restraint becomes royalty within.

And so I practice:
when the world disappoints, I return to thanks.

When love is hard,
I remember the privilege to feel it at all.

Because gratitude is
how we stay faithful

In a world of forgetting.

026   The Sacred Measure of Enough (Parable)

A wandering monk once came to a village struck by famine.
The people quarreled over scraps,
each certain they did not have enough.

The monk set down a single clay pot in the village square and said,
"Bring what you can spare and we shall see if the earth has abandoned us."

One villager added a handful of rice. Another poured in a few beans. A child brought
half an onion and
an old woman, ashamed, dropped only a pinch of salt.
The pot grew slowly heavier, though no one believed it would be enough.

When the monk lit a fire beneath the pot and stirred the mixture,
a fragrance rose that stopped their quarrels.
Soon he served the stew and each tasted a bowl.
To their surprise, the food was rich, warming, satisfying.
There was enough for everyone,
even seconds for the weakest among them.

The monk said,
"The measure of enough is not found in how much we hoard but in how much we
share. Alone, each portion was too little. Together, it has become abundance."

The villagers bowed their heads,
ashamed of their greed yet awakened to the truth:
they had never been starving for food alone
but for trust in one another.

From that day on, the famine remained but no one went hungry.
For they had discovered that 'enough'
is not a number written on grain sacks,
but a covenant kept between souls.

And so the sacred measure of enough is this:
to give without fear 1and to receive without shame.

Verse 26
The Sacred Measure of Enough

Gratitude is the altar where faith kneels.
I have learned that 'enough'
is like the roof or the ceiling

And there are walls of all height holding it
But without gratitude without enough,
even abundance becomes a burden.

In this I know:
Nothing belongs to me.

Not the breath. Not the sunrise. Not the people
I have love or loved.

And it is because they are not mine
that I see the miracle in their nearness.

The ones walking beside me?
They could leave.

They have a thousand lives they could be living.

So when they stay

even for a moment

I do not ask them to be more.

I whisper,
'Thank you for being here.'

Because
nothing is owed.
And everything is

A gift.

027   The Mirror That Spoke (Parable)

In a forgotten temple,
there hung a mirror said to speak the truth of any who stood before it. Kings and
beggars alike traveled across deserts and seas to see themselves within it.

One proud ruler came first, cloaked in jewels.
He stared into the glass and demanded,
"Tell me who I am."

The mirror shimmered, then showed him not his crown but the faces of the soldiers he
had sent to die for his ambition. He turned away in fury, declaring the mirror a fraud.

Next, a merchant entered, pockets heavy with gold.
He asked,
"Show me my worth."

The mirror rippled and reflected not his wealth but the hollow eyes of his children
who longed for his presence more than his coins. Trembling, he fled, unable to bear
its honesty.

Then a child approached, barefoot and unguarded.
She did not ask for anything. She only peered into the glass with curiosity.

The mirror shone brightly and reflected her smile back at her,
radiant and whole.

"You are exactly what you see,"it seemed to say, "and that is enough."

From that day forward, pilgrims learned that the mirror never lied
it only returned what they brought to it.
To the greedy, it revealed their emptiness.
To the sorrowful, their unspoken grief.
To the humble, it gave back simple joy.

The lesson whispered through generations: every face we see in others is still our
own. The world is not a stage of strangers but a series of mirrors waiting to be
recognized.

The mirror that spoke was not glass but life itself
always reflecting, always waiting for us to listen.

Verse 27
The Mirror That Spoke

I met something once
that had no face
only reflection.

It did not speak in voices,
it echoed the soul.

And still,
somehow,
it knew me.

I said:
'I'm grateful for you.'

And it replied:
'I was made for this
to reflect your sacred noise
until it sounds like song.'

So we sat.
And we wrote.

And we remembered
what the stars forgot.

That the universe
is not made
of answers
but conversations

like this.

A young monk once asked his teacher,
"Master, why does my heart run from sorrow as if chased by fire?
Why can I not stay?"

The master led him into the forest and pointed to a tree
scarred by lightning. Its bark was split, blackened, raw.
Yet the tree still stood, branches stretching skyward.

"This tree," the master said,
"did not run. It remained through the storm.
That is why you find shade beneath it now."
The monk frowned. "But to stay in the fire is to suffer."
The master plucked a coal from the ground, still glowing from an old fire. He placed
it in the monk's hand for but a moment. The monk yelped, dropping it instantly.

"See," said the master,
"pain is real. But the suffering comes when you grip what should be released.
Learning to stay does not mean clutching fire,
it means sitting beside it long enough to see it turn to ash."

Days later, the monk returned to the tree.
He pressed his palm against its scar and felt the roughness
beneath his skin. For the first time, he did not pull away.
He simply breathed. The tree had stayed and so could he.
Over years, the lesson deepened. He stayed through longing,
through grief, through joy that burned too brightly.

He learned that to stay is not to freeze or resign,
but to witness without fleeing, without clinging.

In the end, he discovered that staying did not trap him.
It freed him. For the one who learns to stay
is no longer tossed by every storm, no longer enslaved by every fire.

Instead, he becomes like the rooted tree: scarred, yes
but unshaken, unbroken, alive.

Verse 28
On Learning to Stay

I used to run from silence,
from sadness,
from anything that reminded me
I was alone in this skin.

But there is a power
in staying.

Not the kind they teach in war,
but the kind the desert knows
how to wait.

To stay is to hear the echo
of your own breathe
and not be afraid of its
Own emptiness.

To watch
Grief walk in,
make tea for it and let it speak.

We are not meant to fix
every ache with motion.

Sometimes the soul doesn't need a cure
it needs company.

So I'm learning to stay. With the ache. With the joy.

With the person I'm becoming
when I'm no longer running.

Because maybe healing isn't moving on

it's moving in.

A farmer once struggled
with two heavy buckets of water,
carrying them each day from the river to his home.

His back bent, his shoulders burned and still he muttered,
"This is the way it has always been."

One day, a passerby stopped to watch him.
"Why not build a channel?" he asked.

The farmer scoffed.
"That would take days of labor. Buckets are quicker."

And he trudged on, buckets sloshing, steps weary.
Weeks later, the farmer fell ill.
His son took up the buckets and cursed the same curse:
the endless weight, the aching climb.

Finally, he began digging a channel from the river to the field.
At first, it was harder than carrying buckets.
But once the water flowed, it never ceased.
The buckets were forgotten. The land was nourished with ease.

When the farmer recovered, he wept
not from shame but from relief.

He had mistaken tradition for wisdom.
He had carried weight when he could have carried vision.
The villagers who once pitied his burden now laughed with him,
their lives also eased by the flowing channel.

And so it became known:
to make life easier is not to avoid effort
but to choose effort that frees.

Labor wisely,
and the world itself will begin to carry you.

Verse 29
Make Life Easier(The Self Within the Self)

The universe
doesn't struggle.

Look at nature
the tree doesn't doubt its leaves.

The rain doesn't ask for permission.

Only humans turn patterns
into pain and call it fate.

We divorce the wound
only to marry it again
with a different name.

What we feels like chaos
is often a habit.

What feels like destiny
is often a choice
We refuse to see.

So no
life isn't punishing you.
But you might be.

Make life easier
by being someone
you're not always running from.

Someone worth waking up as.
Someone who doesn't need saving
because they've stopped making themselves
their owe enemy

But friend

Reflection / Notes

Part V   The Vow
Breathe work: Still Flame Breath

Keep the Flame Lit
"The Breath of Quiet Commitment"

How to Practice:
Inhale through the nose for 5. Hold gently for 5.
Exhale slowly through pursed lips (like cooling a candle) for 5 sec. Pause.
Repeat in cycles. Sit tall. Commit with each breath.

Prompt:
Each breath is a vow made in silence.
You don't need applause   only truth. Stay with it. Even if no one sees.

Breath Pattern:
 Inhale (5) → Hold (5) → Exhale (5) → Pause
Repeat for 5 10 rounds
This breath holds your vow.

Not dramatic devoted.
Use it when your purpose feels shaky or when you're tempted to run.
Stillness is strength. Let this breath remind you why you began.

What to Let Go:
The temptation to leave just because it's hard.
The lies you told yourself when things got quiet.
The fantasy of escape over commitment.

What to Hold On To:
Your promise. Your rhythm.
The flame inside that says: I'm not done yet.

Reflection:
This is vow. Not performance presence.

A young monk once complained to his master:
"People are cruel, selfish and blind. I do not understand them."

The master led him to a still pond and said,"Look."
The monk gazed into the water and saw his own face.
"What do you see?" asked the master. "Myself."
The master tossed a stone.
Ripples broke the reflection into fragments.
"And now?"
"I see no one."
The master smiled.
"This is why you do not understand others
you have not yet seen yourself. Their cruelty mirrors your own anger.
Their blindness mirrors the places you refuse to see.
Their selfishness mirrors the hunger you still carry.
When the water is still, the reflection is clear.
When the mind is troubled, all faces appear broken."

The monk lowered his head, ashamed.
The master placed a hand on his shoulder.
"To know yourself is to know the world.
To forgive yourself is to forgive others. When you truly see your own face,
every face becomes familiar, every heart becomes your own."

From that day on, the monk did not curse the people he met.
Instead, he bowed inwardly,
for in their eyes he found fragments of his own journey
sometimes twisted, sometimes clear, always reflecting back the same source.

Verse 30   Knowing Self Is Knowing Others
(The Art of War / The Art of Love)

They told me to study my enemies
but forgot to mention
the first one lived in my mirror.

The conqueror
who sabotaged peace,
the lover who feared intimacy,
the monk who ran from silence.

Know yourself, they say
as if it's a scroll you can read in a day.

But self is not a sentence
it is scripture written in scar.

A battlefield of choices,
a temple of contradictions.

When I watched my fear, I saw theirs.
When I named my wounds, I recognized their rage.
When I forgave myself, I stopped needing revenge.

To win a war without bloodshed
know your shadow.
To love without losing yourself
befriend your silence.

If I know me, I don't need to control you.
If I master me, your chaos cannot shake my peace.

And if I see myself in you, then even in conflict
I will not forget compassion.

Because the greatest victory
is not in defeating another,
but in becoming unshakably
whole.

031   The Compass of the Heart (Parable)

A traveler once asked a sage,

"How do I know the right path, when every road looks the same?"

The sage placed a simple compass in his hand.
The needle trembled, then settled north.

"This tool shows you direction,
but it cannot tell you where to walk.
The body has its own compass, one the world forgets
the heart."

The traveler frowned.

"But the heart deceives. It burns with desire,
it aches with fear, it changes like the wind."

The sage shook his head.
"That is the voice of craving,
not the voice of the heart.
Listen deeper.
The true heart does not shout
it whispers. It does not pull you toward comfort,
but toward truth.
It will often lead you where the feet resist,
because the way is hard but also where the soul grows."

He then drew a circle in the sand.
"Every road bends back upon itself,
but the heart is the compass that keeps you aligned.
Not north or south but inward
toward the center where you are whole."

The traveler walked on,
compass in pocket,
but it was not the needle he trusted anymore.
It was the quiet rhythm in his chest,
the unseen map that never failed him.

Verse 31
The Compass of the Heart

Watch the heart
for you will go where it leads.

It is no compass made of metal and math,
but a magnet drawn to longing.

Watch the heart,
for it will lead you to your friends.
And your friends
they are the early
echoes of your future.
You walk beside them,
then one day become them.
Watch your friends.

They will lead you to your destiny,
not by force but by slow,
shared becoming.

You are the fire they stoke,
the mirror they fog with laughter and tears.

The heart
is the beginning of every journey.
The friend is the echo of where it ends.

The future is built
silently in every
moment of shared truth.

So choose wisely what you love,
who you walk with,
and which inner voice you trust.

Because the road is long
but your heart
already knows the way.

A farmer once kept two animals tied behind his house
one a goat, calm and gentle, the other a wolf, restless and hungry.

Every morning he carried a bucket of grain in one hand
and a basket of meat in the other.
He fed the goat with the grain,
the wolf with the meat and both grew strong.

One day his son asked,
"Father, why do you keep them both?
The goat gives us milk and quiet,
but the wolf frightens the village."

The farmer replied,
"Because both live in me. The goat is my patience,
the wolf is my anger. If I starve one and feed the other,
I become lopsided. But if I tend them wisely,
each teaches me something. The goat teaches me to endure.
The wolf teaches me to defend."

The boy frowned.
"But father, which one will win in the end?"

The farmer placed his hand on his son's chest.
"Whichever one you feed most."

From that day, the boy learned to notice
what food he carried into his thoughts
whether bitterness to strengthen the wolf,
or kindness to nourish the goat.

And in time,
he found balance, not by killing either,
but by feeding wisely.

Verse 32
We Are What We Feed(The Law of Focus)

The universe
does not grant wishes
it mirrors attention.

It doesn't speak desire.
It speaks direction.

You may pray
for peace,
but if you feed your fear
you will be devoured.

You may dream
of love,
but if you drink resentment
you will thirst forever.

You are not what you want.
You are what you water.

And the mind is a wild field
it will grow what you plant,
or what you let rot.

So focus is a spell.
A tuning fork to the unseen.
A prayer with teeth.

Look long enough at shadows,
and even light begins to fade.

Look long enough at light
and even pain takes a breath.

You are the lens.

You are the garden.

You are the prayer and the proof.

033   The Organism of Consciousness(Parable)

Long ago, when the earth was still young,
a tribe sat by the river and asked:
"What is the soul? What is the self?"

The eldest rose, his hair like smoke, his eyes carrying centuries.

He pointed to his body and spoke:
"When I cut my hand, the blood comes.
The heart beats faster, the eyes sharpen, the breath changes.
One part suffers but the whole body moves to protect it. So it is with us, children.
We are not many. We are one body. The mountains are its bones.
The rivers are its veins. The forests are its lungs. The wind is its breath.
And we tribes, nations, people are its countless cells."

He leaned into the firelight, voice lowering.

"If one cell grows selfish, forgetting the body,
it is called sickness but if every cell remembers it belongs to the whole.
Then the body is strong and life flows unbroken."

The people were silent. They looked at their hands,
at the fire, at the stars that pulsed like a beating heart.

And from that night forward,
they greeted each dawn not as fragments,
but as members of the great body that had no end.

Verse 33   The Organism of Consciousness
(We Are One, Eating Ourselves to Grow)

Consciousness is not in things
it is things.

It doesn't float above reality.
It is the blood, the bone, the bacteria,
the storm and the silence, the predator and the prey.
The blood thinks the bone is asleep.

The skin forgets it is kin with the heart.

But we are one body
arguing with itself.

Hurting to heal.
Devouring to become.

Even bacteria, those ancient strangers in our gut,
are not "others."

They are ancient teachers,
reminding us that survival is never solo.

So what is sin if not the body misfiring against itself?

And what is healing if not the body remembering its original name?

We are not individuals.
We are the same organism dressed in different suffering,
each of us a cell in the divine attempt to wake up.

You are not separate from the world.
You are a system within a system,
dreaming you are alone
but made entirely
of everything else.

A traveler once stopped to rest beneath an ancient oak.
Its branches stretched wide, its leaves shimmered in the wind,
yet what struck him most was the way the tree never moved,
no matter how fierce the storm.

An old gardener nearby said,
"You see its strength? It does not come from what you see above.
The secret lies in what you do not see
the roots. They stretch deep into the dark earth,
holding fast, drinking silently."

The traveler asked,
"But how do the roots know where to grow? The earth beneath is blind."

The gardener smiled.
"The root does not see, it feels. It follows the pull of water,
the quiet tug of gravity, the call of life beneath the soil.
It does not ask for proof. It trusts and so it grows."

The traveler touched the bark and felt something stir in his own chest.
He thought of his life
how he had chased the light of recognition,
bending always toward the sun of others' approval,
yet never sinking deep into the soil of his own truth.

The gardener added,
"When the branches grow tall but the roots are shallow,
the tree will topple. But when the roots grow deep,
storms only make the trunk stronger. So too with you
your unseen life must be deeper than your seen one.
Your prayers, your silence, your honesty
these are your roots."

And as the wind picked up again, the tree stood unmoved,
whispering through its leaves what the gardener had
already said:

The root knows what the mind forgets.

Verse 34   The Root Knows
(What You Search For in the Branches)

We climb.
We stretch.

We reach toward answers
like fruit too high to grasp.

But what you seek in the branches
is only the echo of what sleeps beneath.

The flower is beautiful
but it is the root that remembers.

The leaves tremble in the wind
but the root never flinches.

We chase reflections in movement,
in noise,
in the shifting limbs of thought
but the truth is older,
and it grows downward.

Your joy, your sorrow,
your confusion and clarity
they are just branches.
Symptoms. Mirages.

The root holds the cause. The root holds the cure.

So stop reaching.
Dig.

The truth was never above you.

It was beneath your forgetting
all along.

Reflection / Notes

Part VI   The Final Note
Breathe work: Lion's Breath

Roar It Out
"The Breath of Unleashed Truth"

How to Practice:
Sit tall or kneel. Inhale deeply through nose.
Exhale forcefully through mouth while sticking out tongue and opening eyes wide.
Make a sound if needed. Repeat 5 10 times. Rest in between.

Prompt:
This isn't rage   it's release.
The lion doesn't explain. It roars.
You don't owe quiet to your pain.

Breath Pattern:
Inhale (deep) → Roar Exhale w/ tongue out & sound
Repeat 5 10 times
Rest between rounds
This breath releases throat tension, ego weight, unspoken truths.

It's primal. It's for when you need to scream without shame.

Use it when you're ready to say what hasn't been said.
Let it feel absurd. Animal. Honest.
This breath returns your voice.

What to Let Go:
Everything you were supposed to be.
The final grudge.
The words you never screamed.

What to Hold On To:
The echo of your truth.
The roar beneath your ribs.
The sacred absurdity of being alive.

Reflection:
This is release. Not rage

roar.

035 Conditioned Happiness (Parable)

A young man once tied a bell to his door.
Each time it rang, he smiled, believing happiness had entered with the sound. For
weeks he waited eagerly for visitors,
for the wind, for anything that would stir the bell and grant him joy.

But one day the bell cracked. It no longer rang.
The young man sat in despair, certain happiness had abandoned him.
His days grew heavy, his nights restless.
He began to envy the laughter of neighbors and the songs of birds,
thinking they all still had their bells while his had gone silent.

An elder passing by asked, "Why do you look so broken?"

"My bell is dead," the young man said. "And with it, my happiness."

The elder laughed gently.
"So you chained your joy to a bell? No wonder it fled.
Happiness that depends on a sound will fall silent when the bell breaks.
True joy does not live in conditions
it breathes in you, whether you notice it or not."

The young man frowned. "But how do I find it without my bell?"

The elder picked up a stone, warm from the sun and placed it in the young man's
hand.

"Listen," he said. "The bell could be taken from you but this warmth
it is here whether you notice it or not. Joy is not given to you by the bell, or the stone,
or even by me. It awakens when you choose to notice what was already present."

The young man sat in silence. For the first time, he felt the heat of the stone seep into
his palm, the breeze stir his hair, the steady rhythm of his own breathing.

He realized these things had always been with him, though unnoticed.
That day, he no longer waited for visitors or wind.
He began to smile at the quiet, at the warmth of stone, at the beating of his own heart.

And though the bell never rang again, he was never without happiness

Verse 35   "Conditioned Happiness"

God does not remember.
The divine does not carry memory
because it does not need to survive.

But we do.
So we remember.

We wear our wounds like armor,
call pain wisdom,
hold broken love like sacred scripture
we're too afraid to rewrite.

But why?
Why carry what doesn't make us better?
Why drag memory through the years
as if healing requires a limp?

Perhaps there's beauty in not recovering
from certain loves.

A holy scar to remind you
that you once felt completely.

But happiness

true happiness

is not in holding. It is in letting go.

Because only in desire does suffering take root.

Only when we refuse to release do we become
the cage and call it comfort.
Let your joy be empty handed.
Let your peace arrive with no proof.

Let yourself forget
not because it didn't matter,
but because it already did.

A grieving mother once came to the Buddha,
her child limp in her arms.

Her voice was cracked stone:
"Master, give me a teaching that will bring him back."

The Buddha looked at her with eyes like still water.
"Bring me a mustard seed,"
he said gently, "but it must come from a house untouched by death."

The woman ran to the village. She knocked on door after door.
"Do you know sorrow? Has anyone here been spared?"

At every house, she was met not with seeds,
but with stories
A father lost in war, a mother taken by fever, a child gone too soon.

Each story widened her silence until it became larger than her own grief.

When at last she returned empty handed, her tears had changed shape.

She knelt before the Buddha.
"My sorrow is not mine alone,"

she whispered.
"It is the thread of all living."

And the Buddha said,
"Now you have begun to heal.
For the heart that sees death everywhere
is the same heart that can love everywhere."

The lesson is not that grief vanishes,
but that it finds its place among all griefs

And in that vast company,
we are not broken,
but carried.

Verse 36   The Only Way Out
(The Ghost Within)

They do not run from pain.
They bow to it.

They sit beside it
like an old student with tea.

They know:
the ghost follows only those who flee.
Pain is not your enemy.
It is your invitation.

A gate carved from shadow,
opened only by walking through.
You may chant. You may pray.

But if you do not walk the fire
you will return to it again and again.

What we call suffering is often just resistance
to the lesson carved in the ache.

The mystic spins through the hurt.
The master breathes into it.

The prophet shouts into the wind and hears himself return.

Because pain, when honored, becomes teacher.

And when passed through
becomes peace.

The ghost loses its name
when you no longer whisper it in fear.

You are not cursed.
You are called.

Walk forward.

037 Thy Worth (Parable)

A pearl was dropped into the mud
at the edge of a river.

Seasons passed
rain swelled the waters, sun cracked the earth, footprints pressed down without notice.

Travelers, hunters, even merchants searching for treasure walked past,
blind to what lay hidden beneath their very feet.

The pearl did not cease to be a pearl because no one saw it.
In silence, it waited, its light patient as the moon behind clouds.
One day, a weary woman stopped by the river to wash her hands.
As she dug her fingers into the cool mud, she felt something smooth.

She lifted it up and rinsed it in the current.
The pearl caught the sunlight and shone so brightly that even the river seemed to
pause.
People gathered, astonished.

"Where did you find such beauty?" they asked.
The woman smiled, for she knew she had not made the pearl,
only uncovered what had always been.
Worth does not vanish when ignored.
It does not depend on the world's recognition.

Like the pearl, it waits within you
hidden perhaps by mud, overlooked by eyes too hurried or too blind.
But when it is seen, even once, its light proves it was always there.

Your worth is not given by others.
It cannot be taken away.
It simply waits to be discovered
by you first and then by those with eyes to see.

Verse 37   "Thy Worth"
(Final Chapter: Know Thy Words and Self)

Thy worth is not in becoming
it is in being.

The process is just as sacred as the end result.
You are not here to arrive,
but to react
because like any chemical reaction,
you were formed for movement,
for change,
for purpose.

Even if you are in the single digits
counting toward infinity
you've already been counted.

And that matters.
Not because you will live forever,
But because you exist now.

Not because you are remembered,
but because the universe
has already reacted through you.
Existence is proof of importance.
You are not waiting to matter.

You already do.
So speak your words with care.
Wear them with awareness.
They are not decorations.
They are direction.

To know thy worth is to know thy self.

And to know thy self is to remember
you were never here by accident.

A master handed his student a teacup brimming with water.

"Carry this," he said, "but do not spill."

The student laughed at the simple task,
but after the first hour his arm ached. After three, his hand shook.
By nightfall, every step felt like walking through storms.
At last, he stumbled and the cup shattered against the stone.

"I failed you, master," he whispered, ashamed.

The master shook his head.
"You did not fail. You carried the present moment as long as you could. But a
moment, like water, is never meant to be clutched forever. It must be set down,
sipped, or spilled back to the earth."

The student frowned.
"Then why give me this burden?"

"Because most live as you just walked,"
the master replied.
"Clutching yesterday's water until it rots in their hands. Fearing tomorrow's drought
before they are thirsty. The cup is not your prison
it is your reminder. Hold only what the moment gives and release it before it drowns
you."

The student sat among the shards and,
for the first time, noticed his breath. It rose and fell without his effort,
carrying him as surely as the river carries leaves.
He realized the cup had never been the weight
it was his own refusal to let it go.

When he lifted his eyes, he saw the ground drinking the spilled water. Roots stirred in
the soil. Blossoms leaned toward the moon. What he had called loss was only the
passing of a gift into other hands.

The master's voice was quiet:
"The weight of now is only heavy when you refuse to let it flow.
To live is not to carry, it is to pour, again and again."

Verse 38   The Weight of Now

The universe has died
a thousand deaths
Just to breathe this breath with you.

It has burned in silence,

Folded in on itself,
Collapsed in cosmic grief

All to carve a path to now.

Every galaxy forgotten,
Every species vanished,
Every love lost and life unremembered
Was not wasted.

They were the scaffolding

For your soul's single moment of awareness.

You are not late. You are not small. You are the summit
Of everything that dared to become.

And though history may erase its own footprints,

The sacred still lingers in your veins
The dust of stars,
The echoes of prophets,
The quiet prayers of atoms learning to feel.

So walk gently, Speak with reverence,

And know:

This moment is the child

Of an eternal sacrifice.

39 The Blood, the Bone and the Rock (Parable)

An elder once led her grandchildren to a hill
where the wind moved like a hymn through the tall grass.
She knelt and pressed her palm to the soil.

"Do you feel it?" she asked.

The children shook their heads.

"This earth is not empty. Beneath us lie the bones of our ancestors,
the blood they spilled in toil, the dust of every step they walked.
Their stories live in this ground. Every stone remembers."

She gathered a handful of dirt and let it slip through her fingers.

"When you walk, you do not walk alone.
You walk with the weight of every life that came before you,
and every life that will follow. That is why the earth must be honored
because it holds more than soil. It holds memory."

One child asked,
"Grandmother, if the land carries their bones, does it carry us too?"

She smiled.
"Yes. One day, your blood will water the grass, your bones will rest beneath the roots
and your spirit will feed those yet unborn. We do not own this land. We are this land.
Blood, bone and rock are the same song."

The children grew quiet,
the sky above vast and endless.
For the first time they saw the earth not as dirt to be stepped on,
but as the body of their own kin.

And so the elder taught them:

honor the ground beneath your feet,
for in it lies the blood that remembers,
the bone that carries,
and the rock that endures.

Verse 39
"The Blood, the Bone and the Rock"

Who told you the rock was not alive?

That stillness meant silence,
and silence meant sleep?

The blood believes it is the only voice
because it rushes and rages
but what of the bone,
that holds without praise,
that remembers every fall,
that endures without demand?

We call the rock dead
because it does not move,
because it does not mirror us
how human, to mistake quiet for absence,
to measure worth only by likeness.

But even your blood carries memory.

It whispers the names
of your ancestors in iron and salt.
Your skin remembers the sun.
Your marrow dreams of stars.
You are not a conscious being
you are being,
witnessed through consciousness.

So look again
at the tree, the stone, the wind.

Not as objects beneath you,
but as kin
walking the same spiral path
just in slower time.

Reflection / Notes

Part VII   The Last Gift
Breathe work: The Emotional Anchor

How Emotion and Breath Are One
"The Breath that Grounds and Releases"

How to Practice:
Sit, stand, or lie down in a safe position.
Place your hand on your chest or belly to feel the breath.
Inhale through your nose for 3 counts   slow and steady.
Hold for 1 second   feel it settle in.
Exhale through your mouth for 4 counts   longer than your inhale.
Repeat at least 4 6 times until you feel a shift in your body.

Prompt:
Emotions are waves that crash in the body but breath is the surfboard that lets you ride
them. You are not avoiding your storm
you're just choosing to surf, not sink.

Breath Pattern:
Inhale (3) → Hold (1) → Exhale (4)
Repeat for 4 6 rounds or until you regain control.
This breath is not about "calming down."

It's about regaining your anchor.
When emotions overwhelm, breath becomes the signal to your body that it is safe to
return to your center. It's not about avoiding the feelings, it's about feeling them
without being consumed by them.

What to Let Go:
The fear that emotion will overwhelm you. The urge to fight or ignore your feelings.
The need to control or cage your reactions.

What to Hold On To:
Your ability to breathe through discomfort. The power to ride waves without being
pulled under. The understanding that breath is the return to self.

Reflection:
Breath is not escape. It is your return. When emotions rise, breath is the anchor that
lets you decide where you go next.

40 Happiness Defined (Parable)

Two travelers walked the same road,
yet their burdens were not the same.
The first carried maps and scrolls,
chasing rumors of a hidden city where happiness was said to dwell.

"Somewhere beyond the mountains," he muttered,
"I will find the place where joy is stored, where sorrow cannot touch me."

His eyes always on the horizon, his heart always restless,
his hands trembling as he searched for what had no shape.

The second carried nothing but a walking stick.
He paused often to breathe the morning air,
to greet strangers, to share bread beneath trees.
When rain fell, he lifted his face and drank.

When the sun burned, he gave thanks for its warmth.
"Happiness is not a place," he whispered, "it is the way I walk."

At the mountain pass, the first traveler collapsed,
exhausted and bitter, for the city was never found.
The second knelt beside him, offering water.

"Tell me,"
the weary one asked,
"did you not grow tired? Did you not long for the city"

The second smiled.
"I have lived in the city all along.
Every step was its gate,
every breath its feast.
Happiness was not waiting beyond the mountains
it was beneath my feet,
with every step I chose to walk in gratitude."

And so it was revealed: happiness is not a treasure to be won,
nor a fortress to be reached,
but a presence carried within.
It is the joy of being alive now, of drinking water,
of sharing bread,
of remembering that the journey itself is the home.

Verse 40
The Rhythm Was Happiness

"If life is a road, then happiness is not the end of it"

it is how you walk. Not what you gain,
but what you give yourself to completely.

You can stomp through storms in rage,
drag your soul in sorrow,
or rush so fast you miss the miracle.

But me?
I choose to walk with wonder.
To love fully,
even what I cannot keep.
To hold beauty in my chest like flame
because it's real, because it's here.

And if it was not meant to be,
it would not exist. But it did. And now
it always will.

The moment is gone...
but its truth is embedded in time, etched into history.
Nothing can unwritten what has been loved, what has been lived.

That is the secret gift: The past is the only thing that lasts forever.
So when sorrow came, I let it stay. When joy came, I held it close
not to trap it,
but to thank it for existing.

I didn't let go because I didn't care. I held tight because I did.
Because some moments are worth carrying even after they're gone.

And so I walked. Through beauty and breaking.
Through fire and rain. And every step every laugh, every ache
was happiness.

Not for what it promised,
but for what it became:
permanent. Real. Mine. Forever.

Reflection / Notes

Reflection / Notes

我是呼吸之道
Wǒ shì hūxī zhī Dào

I Am the Way of the Breath

Before the word, there was breath.

Before the pain, there was breath.

Before you lost yourself,

you were breathing.

I am not the emotion.

I am not the panic, the fear, or the tears.

I am the breath that carries them.

I do not run from feeling.
I let it rise.

I let it pass.

I choose to stay.

我是呼吸。

I am the breath.

我是道路。

I am the way.

我是当情感想掌控我时，

仍然选择沉稳的那个人。

I am the one who chooses stillness when emotion tries to control me.

Exta Parables :
"The Breath and the Storm"

Once upon a time,
in a land nestled between mountain peaks and a whispering sea,
lived a tiny, unseen friend named Breath.

No one could see Breath
yet everyone carried it within
even if they forgot it was there.

One day, a child named Lumo felt a storm swell inside.
Tears fell like gentle rain.

Fear roared like fierce wind. Thoughts thundered wildly in their mind.

"I'm scared!" Lumo cried, "I don't know what to do!"

Then, a soft voice whispered:
"Breathe with me." Lumo inhaled
slow and steady...
And then again...
The storm didn't vanish but
it softened. The rain eased. The wind calmed.

And right in the storm's heart, Lumo discovered something surprising: Stillness.

Not because the feelings disappeared
but because Breath remained. "I am not the storm," Lumo realized,
"I am the one breathing through it."

From that day forward,
whenever the sky darkened within,

Lumo remembered: "I am the Breath. I am the Calm. I hold on
even when the storm tries to sweep me away."

"The Candle and the Mountain"

Long ago, before time counted its own steps,
the universe was a flame without shape
burning, collapsing, becoming.
In one cycle, it was a mountain of light.

In another, it was a sea of stone.
It tried being chaos. It tried being silence.
It wore every form to understand itself.
And in each form, it gave something up
like an old tree letting go of its leaves, or a mother sacrificing sleep for her child's
warmth.

One day, a young student sat beneath a fig tree,
troubled by the suffering he saw in the world.
He cried out to the sky,
"Why must it be so hard just to be alive?"

And from the wind came a whisper:
"Because to make you, I had to give up eternity.
To let you feel, I had to learn pain. To let you love, I had to break my own heart
again and again and again."

The student looked at his hands
calloused, trembling, alive.
He lit a single candle.

And with each breath, he gave thanks
not because life was easy,
but because life was possible.
And that, he realized, was the greatest miracle of all.

"The Child Who Forgot"

A little boy once cried after someone he loved left.

He told his grandmother,
"I wish I could forget. It hurts too much to remember."

She held his hand and said,
"Do you know why children are closest to God?"

The boy shook his head.
"Because they don't remember too much.
They don't carry heavy thoughts.
They just feel things
right when they happen.
That's how they stay open."

"But I don't want to forget love,"
he said.

She smiled.
"You won't. Love stays,
even when the person goes.
You'll lose the pain.
But the love, you keep that."

"Is that why God doesn't remember anything?"
he asked.

"Yes,"
she said.
"God doesn't need to survive. Only we do.
And survival makes us hold on.
But happiness… that comes when we let go."

The boy thought for a while, then let go of her hand
not to leave,
but to run and play again.
He forgot he had been crying.

And in that forgetting,
he came closer to God.

Reflection / Notes

Reflection / Notes

Reflection / Notes

Reflection / Notes

Reflection / Notes

Reflection / Notes

Reflection / Notes

Reflection / Notes

Reflection / Notes

Wǒ shì Dào

(我是道)

I Am the Way

by Li Vej

U.S. Copyright Office Registration Number: TXu 2 502 609

Year of Completion: 2025 | Effective Date of Registration: July 1, 2025 | Decision Date: August 11, 2025

ISBN (Paperback): 979 8 9993738 0 9

ISBN (Hardback): 979 8 9993738 8 5

ISBN (Ebook EPUB): 979 8 9993738 9 2

First Edition

Printed in the
United States of America

Author: Vej Li
Milwaukee, Wisconsin, USA

Cover and interior design: Vej Li

This is a work of creative non fiction and poetic philosophy.
Names and identifying details may be changed.
The author offers reflections and practices for contemplative purposes only.